A Beginners Guide To Backyard Beekeeping

(2nd Edition)

Christopher Selby

Copyright © 2015 Christopher Selby

All rights reserved.

ISBN-13: 978-1511604390
ISBN-10: 1511604395

Table of Contents

Acknowledgements i
Introduction 1
Getting Ready For Bees 3
Beekeeping Equipment 11
Your Bees and Hive 19
Honey 27
Swarms 33
Troubles 39
Colony Collapse Disorder 47
Appendix One Dealing With Bee Stings 53
Appendix Two Fun Facts About Bees 57
Appendix Three: Honey Facts 61
Frequently Asked Questions about Beekeeping 63
Glossary 69
Conclusion 73
About The Author 77

Acknowledgements

To my wife, Elizabeth, who has endured far too much as I pursue my varied interests and follow my dreams, and to Lily and Jake, our curious and inspiring twins, who are a constant source of wonder.

Introduction

Thank you for purchasing my book, "A Beginners Guide to Backyard Beekeeping". I hope you will find it to be an easy to read and follow introduction to the exciting world of backyard beekeeping. I'm sure you will come to enjoy this fascinating hobby as much as I do.

Apiculture, or raising bees is becoming more and more popular as a hobby. People everywhere are discovering the benefits of raising bees at home. A backyard beehive can provide more than enough honey for the average family. Bees also help pollinate plants and flowers and can improve your garden's yield! These are just a few of the benefits that you can expect from your own beehive.

Beekeeping is often mysterious to the newly interested, with this book you will come to understand the basic concepts and practices that are integral to successfully raising bees. Learn about the behavior of bees and how to safely work with them, what you need to set up your hive, how to extract honey and year round tips for caring for your bees and much more!

If you are thinking about raising bees or just interested in this fascinating hobby, "Backyard Beekeeping: A Basic Guide will show you everything you need to get started.

Begin a totally unique adventure in backyard beekeeping today!

Thanks again for buying this book, I hope you enjoy it!

CHRISTOPHER SELBY

Getting Ready For Bees

The collection of honey is probably the number one reason most people become interested in taking up the hobby of beekeeping. While this is reason enough, all its own, honey is the not the only benefit of raising and keeping bees. Recently, another compelling reason to join the beekeeping community has come into the focus of the media's spotlight.

As you most certainly know, the bee population is diminishing at an alarming rate, and no one is really sure why. Colony Collapse Disorder is the name given to this phenomenon, its cause and the extent of its damage probably won't be known for quite some time. Bees are a vital part of the local ecosystem and are largely responsible for pollinating plant life in an area that extends a few miles from the hive. Fewer bees mean fewer plants and fewer plants means less food and less food means more trouble, not just for bees and animals, but for humans as well. Bees and the work they do are vitally important to all life on the planet and many scientific minds are of the opinion that if bees become extinct, human beings are sure to follow.

While it would be misleading to say that becoming involved in backyard beekeeping is going to be single-handedly responsible for restoring the bee population and offset the effects of CCD, but it certainly can't hurt. As the bee population shrinks, each and every hive becomes more important. By engaging in backyard beekeeping, you are more than doing your part to help save the bees and ease the negative impact humanity has been inflicting on the planet.

Aside from the intangible benefit of taking responsibility for your impact on the environment and doing your part to mitigate it, beekeeping affords you the opportunity to see up close and become intimately familiar with these fascinating insects. The world of bees is both alien and familiar at the same time and getting to know and interact with these fascinating creatures would be worth the effort even without the promise of honey and the other bounties of the hive.

Your bees will also have a positive impact on your local plant life, and if you have a garden or a few fruit trees, your bees will help increase the yield of your garden by facilitating pollination.

Beekeeping is a rewarding hobby that provides you with fresh, superior grade honey and has a positive impact on the environment; everyone wins with beekeeping!

A Brief History of Beekeeping

People have been raising and cultivating bees for their honey, wax, and other products for approximately forty-five hundred years and gathering honey from wild bees for about fifteen thousand years. The ancient Egyptians were among the first to try and cultivate bees. They encouraged bees to nest in hollow logs or baskets and used smoke to placate the bees while they removed the honey. These early attempts were little more than crude smash and grab tactics that left a lot of room for improvement.

This simple and primitive method of raising bees was used, virtually unchanged, for a very long time. While it allowed for the systematic collection of honey and made the practice of beekeeping possible, this method often requires that the hive be destroyed in order to collect any honey, wax or royal jelly. While not the ideal way to obtain these things, it was common practice for many years. These types of hives are known as "fixed comb hives".

Fixed comb hives don't have much to offer to the backyard beekeeper or any beekeeper for that matter.

It wasn't until the 18th century when honeybees were first seriously studied by European scientists that substantial advances in the field of beekeeping were made.

Various natural philosophers began to study both the physical structure of the beehive, as well as the behavior and social structure of the bees themselves. Bees were studied under microscopes, dissected and scientifically observed in specially constructed glass chambers- something that had never happened before.

For the first time in human history, bees were starting to be understood. Up until this time, no person has ever witnessed the inner working of the hive or attempted to apply these findings to beekeeping in a practical way.

The knowledge they obtained from their observations lead to major advancements in the way bees were kept and cultivated. The biggest change was to the design of the man-made hive. For the first time in history, people were able to procure honey from a beehive without destroying it. This was a huge leap forward in the relationship between humans and bees, no longer were people predators who stole the contents of the hive by smashing it open and ripping out the contents while keeping the bees paralyzed with smoke and fire. A more symbiotic relationship began to emerge- one where people became more like shepherds than hunters. From now on, beekeeping would focus on the health of their hives and providing, as much as possible, an environment that was supportive of honey production.

These new hives, while still primitive, featured removable slats of wood that allowed the bees to build their honeycombs in such a way that allowed for the beekeeper to get easily inside the hive with minimum disturbances to the occupants. These types of hives are called "top bar hives" and are still in use today.

Further refinements to this design were made by Lorenzo Langstroth in the eighteen hundreds. He introduced movable combs that would easily slide in and out of the hive, making it simpler than ever to keep an eye on the bees and harvest the honey.

Langstroth's design proved so effective that it is still popular today and forms the basis for modern hive design. These types of hives are still referred to as the "Langstroth Hives". They are also called "Movable Frame Hives" and are still the most popular and best choice for the hobbyist beekeeper.

Innovation in hive design has not stopped. New hive designs are emerging. The next evolution in hive design is called the "Flow Hive" and allows for a beekeeper to procure honey in a completely non-destructive and minimally invasive way. Using flow hives, the honey is removed through a tap, much like on a beer or soda keg. Some of these designs are almost competently self-maintaining and makes beekeeping and having fresh honey easier than ever.

As of this writing, there are a few commercially available models of flow hives. This type of low effort beekeeping can potentially bring the practice of beekeeping within the reach of nearly anyone. It is still a new technology and holds a lot of promise and potential. They do tend to be expensive at the moment, as they are still very new to the market. These hives are a great choice for the total novice who can afford to be an early adopter of new technology.

Getting Ready for Bees

Before we get started discussing what you'll need to know to get started in beekeeping it is worth mentioning that if you or any member of your family have allergic reactions to bee stings, you should consider another hobby. Bee stings are a part of beekeeping; there is no way around it. While this poses no real threat to someone without allergies, it can easily become an issue for someone with them.

Preparing yourself and your property for beekeeping, while not difficult, requires some forethought and planning. Before going any further, the first thing to do is check your local laws and regulations regarding beekeeping in your area. While perfectly legal in most areas, the practice is forbidden in some places. Before you move forward with finding a good spot for your hive, spending money and explaining your new hobby to friends and neighbors and all the other preparations you'll need to make, it's best to make sure you are not running afoul of local ordinances.

Speaking of your neighbors, consider letting them know about your plans for beekeeping. There is something alarming about a bee hive appearing out of nowhere, your neighbors will have to deal with your new hobby to a certain extent, and it's only common courtesy to give them a little heads up. You may have some questions to answer, and a few bee myths to straighten out, doing so before you get started is almost always a good idea.

Once you have the legal go-ahead, you're ready to pick out a space for your hive. When choosing where to keep your bees, keep in mind these following considerations:

The Bees will need to be close to a source of fresh water. A nearby pond will work just as well as a gallon container.

Position the hive so that it is protected from the wind and can bask in the morning sun.

Make sure there are no sources of stagnant water around.

Place a barrier between the hive and any potential disturbances (street, walkways, yards etc.) Make the barrier high enough so that when your bees fly up and over it, they are out of the way.

If you paint your hive, don't use toxic paint. Black is a good color for temperate and colder climates and white is fine for warmer areas.

If you plan to place your hive in your backyard, make sure that both you and the bees have enough room.

Your hive can be easily housed on your rooftop, and your bees will be quite happy there if your yard can't accommodate them.

Now that you have made sure that you can legally raise bees without a negative impact on your social standing and have surveyed your property to find an ideal spot for your new hive, the next thing is to consider the equipment that you will need. The first year as a beekeeper requires the biggest investment. Don't be put off by the total amount of your start up expenses. Many of the things you need will only have to be purchased once and will last for many years.

For example, you won't be buying new protective gear or hives year after year. After you have the basics, you only really need to replace you bees (sometimes just the queen) every few years. Of course, there is optional equipment, like specialized machines to make harvesting honey easier, but they aren't necessary for a small operation. The next chapter will provide

Beekeeping Equipment

What do you need to raise bees at home? Thankfully not much. The following list contains the vital items you will need to establish your hive and help it through its first year.

Hive

It is recommended that you get a Langstroth type hive as these are the easiest to deal with and provide the most amount of honey from your bees. The drawback to any hive is the price; a hive kit can cost around $150-200 and a fully assembled hive can run around $200-300.

The standard Langstroth hive consists of several stackable and removable parts. It looks confusing at first, but after reading this description a few times and studying the diagram, it will start to make sense.

The Langstroth Hive

Starting at the bottom, we have the stand. It is important that your hive be elevated so that it won't come in contact with stagnant or standing water. This also helps keep the hive away from skunks and other intruders.

You may want to place the hive on an elevated platform made from cinder blocks and planks of wood. You'll be removing parts and shifting things around, so having the hive a little higher off the ground makes it easier on yourself physically.

The bottom board and the deep super are next. The bottom board provides a base for the hive and a way for the bees to get in and out. The deep super is where the bees will live and work. It's the main living space of your hive. On top of the deep super is placed the "queen excluder", which keeps the queen out of the area where the honey is stored. Atop the excluder, the honey supers are placed. This is where the bees build combs and deposit and store honey. The bees build combs on removable screens, which allows you to take them out and harvest the honey without destroying anything. The honey supers are covered with two lids, known as the inner cover and the outer cover. These protect the inside of the hive from rain, etc.

There are a few more parts to the hive, like the brooding chamber (where the queen stays) and the bee escape (built into the the top covers), but this basic description will do for now. As you assemble or build your hive, you'll come to know all its parts well before your bees arrive.

Top Bar Hives

A Top Bar Hive looks a lot like a mailbox or drawer. The bees live inside, and the hive is covered with wooden slats. The bees build their honeycombs on these slats, which you can easily remove. Top Bar Hives also produce less honey, though many people are of the opinion that the honey is of a higher quality than that produced by bees in a Langstroth type hive.

This type of hive is a good choice for urban beekeepers or those dealing with space issues. It requires less space, less special equipment, and less physical labor. These advantages are the trade-off for being able to harvest substantially less honey, of course because they are smaller and more versatile, it may be possible to have a few Top Bar Hives.

What type of hive you choose is up to you, both types have their supporters and detractors. The pluses and minuses of each hive type aren't as important as which is a better choice for you and your circumstances. Many beekeepers eventually try both types of hive and may flip back and forth between them. The point here is that it is more important to raise your bees than it is to fret over which type of hive is better, Langstroth or Top Bar?

If you are handy with tools, you may be able to save some money by building your hive from a plan. A quick internet search will provide more than a few options for free and commercially available bee hive plans. The hive is the cornerstone of your beekeeping project, so don't try and cut any corners. It's a one-time purchase that will repay you in honey and hours of enjoyment.

Smoker

After the hive, a good smoker is the most important thing that you will need. A smoker is a metal can, attached to bellows. Inside you will burn pine needles, cotton, smoker fuel or anything that will burn slow and produce a lot of smoke. A good one can be had for under $50, at the time of this writing.

Smoke is a beekeeper's best friend and helps you protect yourself from the bees in two main ways. Bees communicate mostly through smell, they release pheromones that send messages to each other. When you spray smoke into the hive, you are essentially removing the ability for them to communicate. This confuses the bees and makes it easier to manipulate them. The smoke also tricks the bees into thinking their hive is on fire. When bees are threatened by fire, they retreat into the hive and eat as much honey as possible. When they are full, they try and fly away to find a new home.

So when you spray smoke on the bees, you are sending them to stuff themselves full of honey and temporarily remove their ability to communicate with each other. They are slow and confused and are less likely to bother you while you harvest honey or perform maintenance.

Hive Tool

A hive tool looks like a paint scraper and is used to separate different sections of the hive and move the bees around. They are inexpensive and should cost no more than $10. If you are planning on using a Top Bar Hive, you won't be needing one of these.

Pith Hat, Mask and Gloves and Protective Clothing

Whether or not you choose to wear an entire bee protection suit is up to you. It is recommended that novice beekeepers wear as much protection as possible until they get used to working with bees and can do so calmly. An experienced beekeeper will often prefer to wear the least amount of protection as possible. This is because he or she knows their bees and is familiar with their behavior. This familiarity eventually will lead to the level of confidence needed to interact calmly with the hive and safely perform routine tasks with less and less gear.

If you choose not to wear the entire get up, you will need a hat with a veil and gloves at the very least. A veil is needed to keep bees from climbing in your ears, up your nose and out of your eyes. Which they tend to do at the slightest provocation. Gloves keep your hands from being stung.

These items are relatively inexpensive, and you should be able to purchase them for under fifty dollars.

Protective jackets and pants average around fifty dollars each.

Other Tools

There are some other things you will need to purchase down the line, but if you have gathered the above you'll be ready to purchase your bees and start your hive. Tools that facilitate the collection of honey have been left off this list since the fist's year's yield is often small and best left to the bees. They will use it as food over the winter, and it will help them strengthen the hive for the second year, when the volume of honey produced increases drastically. You'll have your hands full getting used to your new hive and its occupants, so worry about the honey the second year and focus on raising strong, healthy bees the first.

Bees

During the winter, no later than mid-February you should begin to search for a source of bees. A local beekeeper is a good place to start; they'll either sell them to you directly or point you in the right direction. You should order your bees early in the winter to insure that you have them by spring. A three pound package will provide you with enough bees for your hive. The package contains a queen bee, workers, and drones.

When your bees arrive, the queen will come in her own separate package. The package should have a cork or plug in it, remove this and replace it with a marshmallow. You then place the queen in the brooding chamber.

The reason this is done is to insure that the rest of the bees will get along with the queen. Chances are they will not have been introduced, by plugging the hole with a marshmallow you will cause the bees to eat it. By the time they finish it, the bees and the queen will have acclimated to each other, and things should be fine. If you just introduce a new queen bee directly to the hive, it most likely will not go well.

Make sure the bees have enough food (there will be a food supply in the box) and spray them with sugar water.

Once you have sprayed the bees, gently shake them into the hive. Reassemble the hive and leave the bees alone for a few days.

Depending on where you live, expect to pay up to a few hundred dollars for your bees.

You should be able to gather everything you need for around $500-600. There are many places selling beekeeping equipment and hives online, most of these places will offer bundles or kits, which may save you money.

Starting the second year, your expenses will go down considerably. Keep this in mind if you faced with "sticker shock" while supply shopping.

Your Bees and Hive

A colony of bees that occupies a single hive can number over eighty thousand! A hive functions much the same way as a human city. There are different types of bees, doing different jobs, all centered on the same goal. Every bee has a job to do, and there is no room for the lazy or those unwilling to work. Every bee must earn his or her keep. Bees are not a species concerned with individuality, and each tends to behave more like a cell in an organism rather than an autonomous, independent entity of its on.

This single-minded dedication to the health and needs of the hive is one of the reasons bees are so fascinating to us humans.

Since a beehive is pretty self-sustaining, you won't have to spend a lot of time or effort monitoring or maintaining it. A properly set up hive will require very little from you.

Inside of each beehive, you'll find three different types of bees. There will be one Queen Bee, Worker Bees, and Drones. Each type has a different set of responsibilities and physical characteristics.

The Beehive has a yearly cycle that you need to become familiar with, especially if this is your first year of beekeeping. By following the bees through their year, you will get to know your bees and the best times to work with them.

In this chapter we'll take a closer look at the types of bees in your hive and follow them through a year, so you'll have an idea of what is involved in raising and living alongside them.

The Types of Bees

Worker - As their name suggests, worker bees do all of the work around the hive. They are always non-fertile females and never mate. Worker bees tend to the Queen, the young, they fly from the hive to gather pollen, protect the hive, make the honey and everything else except for mating and egg laying. Worker bees are born from fertilized larvae and make up a majority of the hive's population. These ladies are the real heroes of the hive and are responsible for keeping everything running smoothly.

Queen - There are two types of Queen Bees, Mated, and Virgin. Mated Queens are those that have mated with drones and whose sole responsibility is reproducing as much as possible. They are the focus of the hive, and while she may be the most important part of the colony, she's not really in charge of much. The Queen Bee's job is to mate with the drone bees and lay eggs; that's it. The queen determines whether each egg she lays will become a drone or worker. She can lay more than her weight in eggs every day, which as you can imagine, keeps her pretty busy.

The worker bees tend to her every need; they feed her, clean her and remove her waste. A hive will have only one mature queen though the workers can make more queens if they need to. For example, a new queen will be created when the current queen ages and needs to be replaced

The queen bee is from a fertilized larvae and fed exclusivity Royal Jelly. Somehow, Royal Jelly allows what would normally be a sterile worker bee to transform into a fertile queen bee. All larvae are fed Royal Jelly on occasion, but queens sustain themselves on it exclusively. This results in her large size and fast growth. It takes a queen bee about three weeks to go from an egg to sexual maturity.

When the queen mates with her drones, she flies up as high as she can and waits for her suitors (the drone bees). The reason for these flights is to make sure only the strongest bees pass on their genetic material. During the mating process, the male is killed, and his genetic material can be stored by the queen for years.

When the population of the hive gets too big, the workers may choose to make more queen bees, who will leave the hive with some worker and drones and establish a new hive at a different location. These newly hatched queens are called virgin queens because they will not mate with any members of that hive. The first virgin queen to hatch will seek out and kill the others since they are no longer needed.

Drones - Drones are male bees whose sole purpose is to mate with the queen. While this may sound enviable to some of you, it's not as good as it seems. For one, if a drone does get to mate with the Queen, she always rips off his reproductive organs when she is done, and he plummets to the ground and dies. If the drone doesn't get to mate, he is chased out of the hive by the worker bees when winter comes. It's hard to say who has the better deal. A drone bee is produced from unfertilized larvae.

The First Year With Your Hive

January And February

Since this is your first year as a beekeeper, all you'll need to do during the winter is make sure you find a source of bees and order them in time for spring. Package bees tend to sell out quickly in all areas of the country, so be sure to order early. This is a good time to study up and learn as much as you can about bees and beekeeping and make the preparations to ensure everything is ready to go in the Spring.

March and April

Your bees should arrive by the end of April, so make sure your hive is in its place, and you have the necessary protective gear. When they arrive, you'll place them in the hive and check up on them in a few days.

You'll want to make sure that the bees are healthy and active and that the queen is busy laying eggs. Make sure they have enough to eat, you may need to supplement their honey supply with syrup or something similar. Perform this check every week or week and a half.

This is the time of the year where the hive builds up its numbers. Bees tend to swarm near the end of this season. Swarming is when most of your bees and the queen leave to establish a new hive. Left behind are a newly installed queen and a small population of workers and drones. Swarming is not a desirable occurrence for the beekeeper. The hive will have to repopulate itself before it can get back to what's important making sure you have honey.

Most hives will not swarm in the first year of being established, this gives you some time before you will have to deal directly with a swarm.

May

As the flowers in your area start to bloom, your bees will become more active. This is the time of the year when they are focused on gathering pollen and producing honey. The hive should have increased in numbers by now and shouldn't need much from you. A weekly checking to make sure they are healthy is the main thing. You might need to add more honey supers if you are using a Langstroth. The first year's honey yield is often rather small, so you probably won't need to add any additional supers the first year.

June - August

This is known as Honey Flow Season and is when the hive is at its peak in terms of population and activity and honey production. Again, keep an eye on the honey supers and add more if they are full. This is the time to harvest honey if you choose to do so.

September - October

During the fall, you'll begin to prepare your hive for the winter. Remove the honey supers and ensure the top supers are full of honey. The bees will need this honey to feed themselves during the upcoming winter season.

November - January

This is the dormant season; the workers will kick the drones out of the hive, and the remaining workers will form a cluster inside the hive for warmth. You should leave the bees alone during this time of the year. The population of your hive will have decreased substantially, this is normal and no cause for concern.

That's about it for the first year of owning a hive. There may not seem like there is much to do, but your role as a beekeeper is that of a monitor, not so much a direct influence on the bees. You just need to check up on them to make sure they are healthy, safe and have enough food and water.

The responsibilities of the home beekeeper do increase during the second year, you'll have to insure your hive is healthy in the spring and harvest the excess honey.

How to Check on Your Bees

When you need to open the hive and check on your bees, wait for a sunny, warm day. You don't want to go out until after the worker bees leave for the day. Once they are gone, put on your protective gear, grab your smoker and hive tool and approach the hive. Don't make any sudden or frazzled movements. Be calm around the bees. Remove the top of the hive, smoke it and perform your checks/maintenance as quickly as possible. Hopefully, everything is OK, and you'll be able to replace the top and leave the bees to themselves in a few minutes.

Make sure you wear light-colored clothing and avoid brown. Wearing brown might make the bees think you are a bear and could anger them. Remember to remain calm, and you'll have nothing to fear and will even start to look forward to checking your hive.

If you are using a top bar hive, checking on your bees is substantially easier. You'll simply lift each slat out, one at a time and check on the bees. You'll still want to smoke the bees first and wear your protective gear.

By now you should have a solid idea of what is involved in raising your own bees. It *really* isn't all that difficult to get started.

Honey

Honey tasted good enough to drive ancient man to devise ways to steal it from bees. Throughout history, honey has been coveted by people all over the world. It was used as a sweetener, a medicine and served as a powerful symbol of wealth that was used by both religions and kings.

Honey was even used as a sacrifice to the gods by the Romans, Greeks, Buddhists and ancient Egyptians. While honey is not the only thing that can be harvested from your hive, it is the most popular. Honey acquisition has always been the driving force behind the desire to raise, study and keep bees.

Honey is just as popular today as it was in the ancient world. It is used primarily as a sweetener, instead of sugar. It also enjoys a rather sketchy reputation as a cure-all miracle food. While there is no disputing that honey is full of health benefits and may have legitimate medicinal uses, it's never a good idea to treat yourself medically, so see a doctor when you need to. The truth is, honey is pretty impressive on its own, its benefits don't need to be exaggerated.

Where Does Honey Come From?

When worker bees bring back flower nectar to the hive, it is chewed by the bees and regurgitated. This process is repeated several times. After the nectar has been mixed with the secretions of the bees, it is stored in wax cells in the hive to be used as food later. This mixture of nectar, bee saliva and time is what produces honey.

When the honey is harvested by a beekeeper, it tends to by crystallized. Think of a soft rock candy. This product is further processed and ends up looking like the supermarket honey we are all familiar with.

What's in Honey?

Nutritionally speaking, honey is comprised mostly of the carbohydrates fructose and glucose, a few minerals, very few vitamins and several powerful antibacterial and antioxidant compounds.

Store bought honey is often pasteurized and filtered in order to ensure its safety. Raw honey, which is what you will be harvesting from your bees, tastes better and has a higher nutritional value than the store bought kinds.

Honey as a Medicine.

The Egyptians knew the value of the antibacterial properties of honey and used it to dress wounds, much the way antibacterial ointments are used today. The Greeks and Romans also praised honey for its curative abilities. Folk medicine attributes a long list of curative properties to honey. The most popular of which involve treating colds and sore throats. Many people swear by tea and honey as a cure for a lost voice. Others claim that apple cider vinegar mixed with honey will shorten a cold. These claims, while interesting, have not been accepted by a majority of medical professionals.

Honey as a Symbol

The easy procurement of honey is a relatively recent phenomenon, in the ancient times it was a rare and valuable - not to mention somewhat dangerous to obtain. It was expensive and not always available. Demand exceeded supply, and only the richer members of society had the means to purchase honey.

To the ancient person, honey was rare, greatly coveted and expensive. This view of honey led to it eventually being used symbolically to represent wealth and naturally became associated with royalty. It was seen as a special food for special people.

Many cultures also have a history of using honey in religious ceremonies as an offering to gods and spirits. This practice is found throughout the world, in religions that have little or nothing else in common.

Honey is used as an offering in some sects of Buddhism and Hinduism. Ancient Egyptian priests were known to use honey as an offering in their ceremonies. In Santeria, Ochun, the spirit of wealth and pleasure is strongly associated with honey. A little research by the curious will turn up a large number of myths and practices from all over the world that involve honey and bees.

While not directly related to the practice of keeping bees, the myths and lore regarding bees and honey is an interesting subject for novice beekeepers to explore.

It seems that the love of honey and using it to represent wealth and plenty is a common thread that runs through all people, regardless of race, geographic location or point in history.

Other Bounties of the Hive

Aside from honey, a bee hive can provide you with beeswax, bee pollen and royal jelly.

Beeswax

Beeswax is secreted from special glands found only on the worker bee. The workers take this wax, chew on it, where it mixes with a little bit of pollen. The bees use this wax as a building material for constructing some of the hives interior structures, such as honeycombs. Honeycombs are used to store honey and pollen and also as a place to raise larvae. The cells that store pollen and honey are capped with wax to preserve and protect the contents.

Beeswax is used by people to make candles, skin care products and is even found in pharmaceutical and cleaning products.

Royal Jelly

Royal Jelly is also secreted from glands which are located on the heads of worker bees. In the hive, it is primarily used to feed the Queen bee. All bee larvae are fed Royal Jelly for the first three days; only the Queen continues to feed on it past that point.

Humans have used Royal Jelly primarily as a health supplement. It continues to be popular despite the fact that the supposed benefits to people have not been verified or supported by health professionals and the FDA.

Bee Pollen

The pollen collected by worker bees ends up being compacted into tiny balls and stored in the cells of a honeycomb. During this process of collecting and storing the pollen, it mixes with honey, wax and bee saliva. This pollen is consumed by the bees and provides them with protein.

Bee pollen, like Royal Jelly and honey, is also said to have curative properties and is commonly used by people as a health sup

Swarms

Swarms: What They Are and Why They Happen

Swarming is the name given to the process by which bee colonies divide. When the population of the hive grows too much, many of the bees will leave and establish a new hive. Those that remain will focus on repopulating rather than pollination and honey making until the population returns to normal.

Swarming mostly happens the spring, though it is a possibility anytime, as long as the hive is not dormant. When the decision to swarm has been made, the preparations begin. Worker bees create larger cells to raise new queens. These cells are called "Queen cups." Since Queen bees are larger than workers and drones, they need to be raised in larger cells. The standard sized honeycomb cells are too small.

While the new queens are maturing, the existing queen stops laying eggs and begins to slim down in order to be able to fly. When the colony is ready to swarm the bees that are leaving fill up on pollen and honey. It's a lot like a large family preparing for a long trip.

Once ready, the bees depart their hive and fly to a nearby safe spot where they stay until an acceptable permanent location is found. Since each bee only has a small amount of food, it is of vital importance that a new hive be established as soon a possible. The longer it takes, the greater chance the bees have of starving to death. They are also exposed to environmental dangers such as intense weather and predators.

Scout bees are then dispatched from the temporary nesting area and go in search of a more stable and permanent spot to make a new hive. When they find a potential spot, the scouts return to the temporary site and perform a dance. If the other scout bees are impressed by this dance, they will go and check it out. This process continues until a new site has been agreed upon. The process can take a few hours to the better part of a week. If all goes right, the colony will be settled in, and the cycle will begin again.

Meanwhile, back at the original hive the new queen bee busies herself replenishing the population of the hive. She will kill any other queen bees that were raised prior to the swarm, and it will soon be business as usual.

While swarming is a natural and necessary part of the life cycle of the honey bee, it does present some difficulties for the beekeeper.

Swarms and Beekeepers

The most obvious drawback to swarming, from the bee keeper's perspective (aside from losing most of his or her bees) is that honey production stops during the process and the beekeeper will most often find him or herself without a drop of honey for that year's efforts.

There isn't much that can be done after a swarm has been cast, save for getting used to the idea that you'll have no honey and need to bolster your remaining bee population and hope for a better time next year.

A first year Queen will probably not be concerned with swarming - there's enough to do to keep the hive busy and the population levels normal. This is good news for the novice beekeeper since you'll have your hands full learning the ropes and getting acclimated to your new hobby. The second year is a different story; the bees are almost guaranteed to cast a swarm.

Because the consequences of swarming are so severe, beekeepers have developed ways of preventing or minimizing them. The earliest forms of swarm control centered around replacing your departed bees by luring in a swarm that has left its hive. This approach is sort of like replacing tenants in an apartment. Now a days the modern beekeeper has more sophisticated methods of managing swarms at their disposal.

Many beekeepers deal with swarms by making sure there are suitable nesting areas nearby and try to anticipate the swarm by giving the bees a place to go that is still manageable by the beekeeper. While this is not as good as your hive not swarming in the first place, you will lose honey production time during the process, it is better than losing a majority or all of your bees.

It is also common practice to clip one of the queen bee's wings. If she is unable to fly, there can be no swarm. If the queen has already mated and is laying eggs, she will not need to make any more mating flights, so her wing can be clipped without interrupting the bee's honey production cycle.

Swarm management is an important part of beekeeping, while not overly complex or difficult it does require planning and knowledge of the behavioral dynamics involved. The techniques center around working with what the bees are naturally going to do and either seek to control the process or short circuit it before the swarm can be cast.

Since swarming is unlikely in the first year, you'll have plenty of time to prepare yourself. The brief overview of the swarming process presented here is meant to familiarize yourself with the basics so that you have a foundation for understanding other, more detailed, sources of information. It is never a bad idea to seek out and talk to more experienced beekeepers in your area and pick their brains about swarms and swarm management.

Swarm Facts

A cast swarm of bees, while terrifying to the inexperienced poses little threat of danger to people. Researchers point to two reasons for this. The first is that the swarm has no young to protect, so they are naturally less aggressive. The second is the bees are exposed and vulnerable to both the elements and predators while they are in between nesting sites.

They are more concerned with their own safety and will tend to avoid any potential difficulties.

Dealing with the occasional swarm in a populated area is an extra source of income for many amateur beekeepers.

A hive can swarm up to five times in one season. This is, thankfully, incredibly rare. It is realistic to expect no more than two swarms per season.

Troubles

So far in this book we have taken a rather rosy approach to the art of keeping bees. This was done, not to lull you into a false sense of how easy, trouble free and fun beekeeping is, but rather to make explaining the basic concepts and techniques involved as easy as possible to explain and understand. In any undertaking, things can and will go wrong - beekeeping is no exception. Bees are subject to several diseases, parasites, and other potential dangers.

This list is by no means comprehensive but highlights some of the more serious and common conditions you are likely to run into while raising bees. Some of these are easily preventable with good habits and hygiene practices, some require your intervention in the form of administering medical treatments to the bees. These diseases are difficult to detect and in many cases, laboratory testing is needed to determine what, exactly, is going on at the root of the issue.

Some of the most common health issues facing bees are:

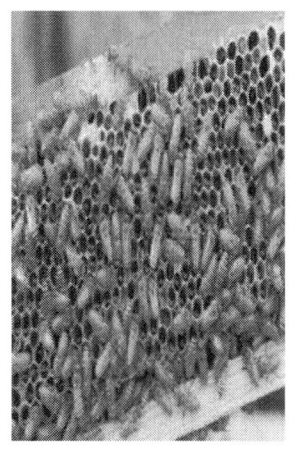

Diseases

American Foulbrood

American Foulbrood is a bacterial disease caused by Paenibacillus larvae, a spore-forming bacteria. This disease targets young bee larvae that are less than twenty-four hours old. It is passed into the bee larvae while eating infected food. Infected larvae will usually die within three days of being infected. The spores do not die, but rather reproduce and can infect the entire hive's young. Paenibacillus larvae spores can live over thirty years, hiding on and in your beekeeping gear and cause reinfection of your hive, making it difficult to get rid of once it has taken hold.

Chalkbrood

Chalkbrood, also known as Ascosphaera apis, is a fungus that takes up residence in the guts of bee larva. Much like a tapeworm in a human's stomach, Ascosphaera apis, eats the food that has been eaten by the larva. It puts itself in direct competition for the young bee's food. Once the fungus has starved the larva to death, it begins to consume the carcass, which turns a chalky, brittle white color.

Most often this is an issue during a spring season with heavy rainfall. More often than not, if the ventilation of the hive is improved, Chalkbrood will clear up without further attention from you.

Stonebrood

Stonebrood is also caused by a fungus known as Aspergillus fumigatus, which is usually found in dirt. Several other types of fungus are also responsible for this condition.

Working in a similar fashion to Chalkbrood, Stonebrood also uses food to arrive in the bee larva's stomach and sets up shop. Instead of stealing the larva's food, the spores are hatched inside the young bee, who soon dies. The corpse becomes black and hard. It is difficult to break or smash the infected bodies, a characteristic which gives this condition its name. The Stonebrood fungus will then encase the body in a fake skin, similar to mummification and reproduce.

Stonebrood is not a guaranteed death sentence to the hive but can be. Odds of recovery depend on how healthy and strong the hive is and the severity of the outbreak.

Aside from bees, this condition may affect other kinds of bugs, birds, and small animals.

Pests

Acarine or Tracheal mites

On the Isle of Wight, in 1904 many of the bees started to die in a mysterious fashion. The condition worsened until most of the bees in the British Isles were gone. The cause of this mass die out was discovered in 1921 to be a parasite known as Acarapis woodi.

These tiny mites take up residence in the airways of the honey bee. They live there and lay eggs for a while and then climb out of the bee's airway and attempt to transfer themselves to a younger bee, where they will begin laying eggs again.

Usually, it is required to send a few dead bees out to a lab to confirm the pretense of these mites. Treating an infection involves using grease and sugar or Menthol.

Nosema

Nosema is also a fungal infection. It targets the intestinal track of adult bees. It is not a serious threat to your hive as long as your bees are able to leave the hive to clean the waste from it and themselves. Conditions such as an extra rainy or cold season and poor hive placement encourage Nosema to take root.

It can usually be resolved by increasing ventilation and removing the honey from the hive. It should be replaced with sugar water

Small Hive Beetle

Small Hive Beetle aka Aethina tumida is originally from Africa.

The beetle is born in the dirt near a hive, makes its way in (much like a fox in a hen house) and does its best to do as much damage to your bees and their hive as possible.

Effective treatments include the use of diatomaceous earth, which kills the young beetles and keeps them from entering the hive. This is a rather new technique but has many supporters who swear by it. Pesticides are also an option but are only used when absolutely needed, bees are very sensitive to pesticides and their use is minimized as much as possible in beekeeping.

Varroa mites

Known in scientific circles as Varroa destructor these mites can be seen unaided on the body of an infected bee and look like a red dot on an infected bee's thorax. These mites target bees in all stages of maturity from pupal up to adult.

Mostly a threat to smaller colonies, these mites help themselves to the bodily fluids of their host until the host expires. Varroa mites are capable of destroying an entire hive and have done a good job eliminating wild bees from several areas of the world. If the infection is too much, the remaining uninfected bees will often leave in search of a new hive.

The condition is often treated with pesticides and barrier methods of pest control, which make it difficult for the mites to get inside the hive in the first place.

Wax Moths

Galleria mellonella or, the greater wax moth feeds on beeswax. It essentially eats away at the inner structures of the hive. Unusually, no intervention is needed to clear up an infected hive. The bees are pretty capable of hunting down and killing wax moths, keeping them from becoming a serious problem. Some beekeepers use moth balls or discs to keep these pests at bay.

Other Unfavorable Conditions

Chilled brood

This is more a result of poor beekeeping habits rather than a proper disease. This condition is caused when the interior temperature of the hive cannot be properly maintained because the hive remains open too long for maintenance in cooler temperatures. This is similar to opening your front door while the heater is on but instead of catching a chill or cold, the young bees (or brood) are prone to deformities or death.

Dysentery

People aren't the only creatures that can suffer from the effects of Dysentery; this serious condition is also a threat to bees as well. It is caused in a hive the same way it breaks out among humans- by living with your own waste. Dysentery outbreaks are possible when it is too cold for the bees to leave the hive to remove their waste. If it is a very cold winter with few warm or warmish days, the bees will not leave and waste piles up, setting the stage for Dysentery to break out.

Many beekeepers attempt to prevent Dysentery by removing the honey from the hive and replacing it with syrup water before the winter. This cuts down on the waste the bees produce and by extension keeps Dysentery out of your hive.

Exposure to pesticides

Bees are incredibly sensitive to pesticides and other commonly used toxic chemicals. Minimize your bee's exposure to pesticides by not using them in your garden, or on your property. There's not much you can do to make other people stop using them, the best course of action is to be aware and try to reduce exposure as much as possible.

Colony Collapse Disorder

Colony Collapse Disorder is a serious and mysterious condition that is at the heart of many a heated debate in the beekeeping community. It will be addressed and explored in a separate chapter.

Other Dangers to the Hive

Bears, Mice in the winter, Toads and frogs, some birds and even skunks pose a very real threat to your honey bees and their hive. Keeping wildlife away from your hive is mostly common sense. It is recommended that you research and become familiar with which threats are viable in your area and employ the same common sense measure you use to keep them away from other parts of your home or property.

In the next chapter, we will discuss the Colony Collapse phenomenon in a little more detail.

Colony Collapse Disorder

Colony Collapse Disorder or CCD is a mysterious occurrence where entire colonies of bees vanish, for seemingly no reason.

A hive that has fallen prey to Colony Collapse Disorder will have no adult bees or adult bee corpses inside. The queen will usually be alive, as will many of the young and the hive will still contain honey. The hive usually contains evidence to support the presence of Varroa mites.

Whatever the cause of CCD is, it only seems to directly affect the adult bees, the hive collapses due to the neglect caused by the absence of adult workers. As you should know by now, it is the worker bees who do everything in the hive. The queen and the drones are only concerned with mating, leaving all the others duties to the worker bees.

While reported cases of Colony Collapse Disorder has been on the rise since October 2006, the condition has been known to beekeepers for a long while now. The first occurrence that was recorded happened in 1869, and it has been given several names over the course of time. Spring Dwindle Disease, Autumn Collapse Disease, Spring Dwindle Disease, May Disease and Disappearing Disease are some of the titles formerly given to this phenomenon.

Experts are at a loss to explain why or how the bees are vanishing. Researchers have found a combination of factors that, when considered together may be an important part of why CCD is becoming more and more prevalent. Some of the major factors thought to be at the root of the current Colony Collapse Disorder epidemic are:

Environmental factors such as, the increased use of pesticides, the constant encroaching of humans upon the natural habitat of bees (and every other animal, for that matter) and the increasing rarity of suitable food sources.

The emergence of several new diseases and an increase in varroa mite infection

Stress. Like people, bees can only do so much before they reach a point of diminishing returns. Also like many people these days, bees are finding themselves working way too hard in exchanges for substantially less than they need in order to survive. The end result is a substantial decrease in the colonies ability to defend itself and maintain its health- both at the collective and individual levels.

The heavy, careless hand of man has altered and polluted the environment in such a short amount of time and to such a great extent that bees have not been able to evolve fast enough to handle them. The continued ruination of the planet is unlikely to stop, or even slow down anytime soon leaving humans to ponder the now very real and imminent threat of bees becoming extinct in the not too distant future.

The total extinction of honeybees spells disaster for the rest of the life on the planet. Bees do more than make honey and ruin picnics - they are solely responsible for pollinating most of the plants which humans and many other living things depend on for food. Just in the United States, bees are responsible for pollinating upwards of 66% of the crops grown for food!

That's just what bees do for people in the United States; the rest of the world is no less dependent on the favors of bees.

Colony Collapse Disorder is already affecting more than your local bee population; the drastic reduction in the worldwide bee population is starting to affect agriculture and other areas of commerce.

Some farmers now rent bees to pollinate their crops, since they can no longer depend on being visited by feral or wild bees. While this solution works for now and has prevented the loss of tons and tons of food, it won't work forever. Unless something can be done in the relatively near future to substantially increase the number of bee colonies and stop CCD, humans the world over will be facing an unprecedented food crisis.

Colony Collapse Disorder is everyone's problem. Everyone needs to eat, and the crazy truth is that bees are primarily responsible for providing us with almost all of the food we eat. Until CCD is properly understood and a cure, treatment or method of prevention is available there isn't much that seems like it can be done. The most sensible strategy is to become more aware of our effects on the environment in general and bees in particular.

Each and every one of us can make a few minor changes in our daily routines and lifestyle that can help reduce the contributing factors of Colony Collapse Disorder:

This should go without saying, but the simplest thing anyone can do to help fight CCD is to simply be nicer to bees. Don't kill them, go out of your way to avoid them and let them have their space. If you can help one escape or find its way back to where it came without hurting it, do so.

The ability for this method to make a positive difference is totally dependent upon these practices becoming widespread. You can do your part to educate others by your example.

If you have a garden, consider some minor additions to make it "Bee Friendly". You can grow flowers and plants that appeal to them. Avoid using pesticides of any kind and rely on non-chemical and organic methods of pest control.

If your property can accommodate it, consider making a few attractive spots for bees to nest. Not so you can harvest the honey - just so they can do their thing. One of the causes of Colony Collapse Disorder is the vanishing of suitable areas for bees to live. Doing what you can to encourage them to nest on your property is a small gesture that can potentially have a large impact.

Become a beekeeper. More beekeepers mean more bees that are able to benefit from the watchful eye of a caring human. The bees that you keep will have several distinct advantages over their wild counterparts.

Become aware of your personal impact on the environment and take some steps to minimize them. There is no need to convert to solar panels or move off the grid or make any extreme changes to your life, but you probably could make a few dozen small ones that will have a positive impact over time. Take a look at your daily routine and see where you can make more "bee friendly" choices throughout the day.

The only way to ensure the future of healthy, strong bee colonies is for everyone to do their part, no matter how small it may seem. Colony Collapse Disorder is a byproduct of how our modern society takes the natural world for granted and uses it up like it will grow back in a few days until this fundamental attitude changes, CCD and all that comes with it is unlikely to get better. The only hope is that people begin to make small changes that add up to make a big difference.

Appendix One
Dealing With Bee Stings

There is no way not to get stung by bees as a beekeeper. They go hand in hand. The good news is that it isn't that much of an issue- as long as you are not severely allergic. If you don't have severe allergic reactions to bee stings, you have little or nothing to worry about.

Bee stings may, well sting a little bit, but they aren't the sort of thing that demands professional medical attention. After awhile, you will probably come to regard bee stings in much the same light as a mosquito bite - nothing more than an annoying part of being outside in the summer.

When you are stung by one of your bees, these first aid tips will help you properly care for the sting:

The first thing to do is to remove the stinger. Use your fingernail, a pair of tweezers or a similarly shaped object to scrape the stinger out of your skin. DO NOT squeeze the stinger and pull it out as this will only serve to introduce more venom into the area.

The second step is to do something to control the swelling. Remove anything (tight clothing, rings etc..) that may constrict the area. If you were stung on the arm or leg, elevating the affected limb is recommended. Apply ice to the area, this will help reduce the swelling.

Now that you've removed the stinger and taken care of controlling the swelling as best you can, you might want to consider over the counter pain medication and a topical anti-itch ointment to alleviate any pain and itchiness.

The sting should be fine in less than a week. Keep in mind that the more you are stung, the less it hurts. Many veteran beekeepers hardly pay attention to an occasional sting. It's considered part and parcel of this otherwise fascinating and rewarding hobby.

The above situation assumes that the person stung is not allergic to bees. To a person with a bee allergy, a sting is a major inconvenience at best and a potential death sentence at worst. If you notice any of the following symptoms, then call an ambulance as soon as possible.

Vomiting, nausea or stomach pain

Difficulties breathing, tightness in the chest or throat.

Becoming dizzy or disoriented.

Excessive swelling or itching in the affected area.

Passing out.

The above steps will help you mitigate any adverse effects of a bee sting. If you are unsure about whether or not to seek medical attention, err on the side of caution and consult your doctor. An ounce of prevention is worth a pound of cure, goes the old saying.

The best way to avoid the ill effects of a bee sting is to minimize your chances of being stung in the first place. These tips will help you avoid being stung:

Wear your protective gear. This is a no-brainer, but it needs to be mentioned. While it is not meant keep you from ever being stung, your hat, gloves, and other protective gear are your first line of defense against being stung.

Always use your smoker. Always.

Wait until after most of the worker bees have left for the day before attempting to work with your hive. A sunny, warm day is the best choice.

Be careful of your attitude. Being scared or trying to rush will lead to making mistakes. Try to stay calm. Make deliberate, confident movements while you go about your work.

Wear light colored clothing.

Again, it should be stated that you will be stung. The above tips will help you keep the amount of times your are stung to a minimum.

The best thing to do is to accept bee stings as part of the process and look forward to the day when you have acclimated to them, and they no longer bother you.

Appendix Two
Fun Facts About Bees

Humans have been captivated and mystified by bees and the way a hive functions for thousands of years. While it is not at all necessary to be an expert on bees in order to be a beekeeper, I'm sure you will eventually find yourself wanting to learn more about these insects and what they are up too. To help get you started learning about bees, here are some interesting facts about them:

Honeybees are not native to North America and were brought here by early European settlers. The first honey bee introduced to the continent was the German Honey Bee.

The population of a beehive during the peak summer months can rival the population of Delaware! When a hive is healthy and at its most productive, it will be home to 80-10000 bees. That number will dwindle by half when winter comes.

Honey bees communicate almost exclusively via pheromones. They use the scent of these hormones to communicate and coordinate with each other. Smoke disrupts this process and temporarily jams the bee's radar, making communication impossible.

The use and consumption of honey by humans is depicted in Ancient Grecian, Egyptian and Stone Age Paintings.

A queen bee can lay around 2000 eggs a day, every day for up to five years. She only mates once, with several males, whom she kills. Their genetic material will still be able to fertilize eggs several months or even a few years after their death!

Honey bees have five eyes and two pairs of wings. Three of the eyes are on the top of the head.

A person would need to be stung over one thousand times in order for bee stings to be fatal.

Bees utilize a form of climate control. When it is too cold in the hive, they form together in a cluster and vibrate their wing muscles to provide warmth. In the summer, they use their wings as fans to cool the hive.

Honeybees are responsible for pollinating about 33% of the food consumed by Americans.

Top speed of the average honey bee is a whopping 15 miles per hour. The wings of the average bee beat about 11,000 times per minute. They tend to fly upwards of three miles from their hive.

Some medical researchers think that bee venom may someday help treat various conditions such as HIV, MS and some types of arthritis.

When an older bee takes over a job usually done by a younger bee, the older bee's brain will start to age in reverse.

No other insect on the planet makes food for people.

Honey will remain fresh and edible for thousands of years.

Honey bees have a pair of stomachs. One for to gather nectar and one to digest food.

Of course, that's not all there is to know about bees. It isn't even all of the interesting things to know about bees. It is hoped that the above list of facts will inspire you to deepen your knowledge of honey bees and all they do for us and our planet.

Hopefully, you want to learn all you can about them. Not only will it make you a better beekeeper, the academic study of bees will also provide hours of enjoyment. As you raise and work with bees, you'll naturally want to learn more about them, as you learn more about them, you'll want to spend more time working with and tending to your hives. When this happens, congratulations! You Officially have "Bee Fever"! Welcome to the club!

Appendix Three: Honey Facts

Honey is just as interesting as the bees that make it. To the bees, honey is just food to fuel the hive and keep it running. To people, honey is much more than a food. It has been used as money, medicine and in religious rites for a very long time. Here are some interesting facts about the golden nectar which has captivated the imaginations and taste buds of people the world over.

In Spain, there is an ancient cave known as the "Cave of the Spider". It's walls depict a painting of a person taking honey from a bee hive. The age of the painting is thought to be around 14-15 thousand years old!

In Germany during the Middle Ages, the working class was permitted to pay taxes with honey and beeswax instead of money.

It takes the nectar from nearly two million flowers and travel well over 50,000 miles to produce one pound of honey.

Honey is such an efficient food for bees that a single bee would only require two tablespoons worth to have the energy to fly all the way around the world.

A single honey bee is almost able to produce a twelfth of a teaspoon of honey in her lifetime.

Honey contains a large amount of antibacterial and antifungal compounds. This means that it doesn't really ever spoil. Archeologists recovered sealed containers of honey from King Tut's tomb, which were over two thousand years old and perfectly fine to eat!!

Roman legionnaires were known to use honey as an ointment for wounds. The antibacterial compounds prevent infection and speed up the healing process.

Ancient Egyptian surgeons used honey to treat and prevent post-surgical infections.

The word "honey" is said to be derived from a Hebrew word which meant to "enchant".

Not all honey is created equal nor does it taste the same. The color and flavor of honey can vary considerably depending on which flowers were used to produce it, the weather and the types of bees involved. Even the type of hive you use can influence how your bee's honey looks and tastes.

The same properties that make honey so useful in preventing infections in wounds and cuts also is also said to make it a fairly effective acne treatment.

There is no doubt that honey is one amazing substance. It has been a part of the human experience almost from the get go. There is also no doubting that honey does have some valid medical uses, but it isn't the place of this book or any other for that matter to make outrageous claims about what honey can do. The information in this book isn't intended to replace the advice of your healthcare provider, and is provided for informational purposes only.

Frequently Asked Questions about Beekeeping

Why Raise Bees at Home?

The most popular reason for keeping bees is honey. The honey that comes from your own beehive is going to taste better and be better for you than store bought honey. Aside from honey, raising bees offers a rare chance to observe and work with these fascinating insects up close and in a way most people will never experience. Bees are also good for local plant life. In many cases, bees are responsible for pollinating plants and flowers. If you have a garden, raising bees can be beneficial to them. If you don't, the local flora will benefit instead. Another good reason is that as bees are becoming more and more scarce, each and every hive becomes more and more important.

How much space do I need to raise a beehive?

The bees themselves don't need that much room. The trick is making sure that the bees don't interfere with what's around them. Make sure they will not disrupt pedestrian or vehicular traffic or bother your neighbors. For those short on space, consider placing your hive on your rooftop.

What species of bees is best for the novice?

There are several species of honeybee available for your hive. The Italian Honeybee is considered the most popular among beekeepers and recommended for beginners. Here are the most popular species:

Italian

These bees are disease resistant and less defensive than most kinds of honeybee. They were brought to the United States in 1859 and quickly became the darling of beekeepers across the nation.

Buckfast

This bee was developed by a Monk in England during the 1920's. During this time, many of the bees fell victim to disease and nearly vanished from the British Isles. This strain was developed to resist disease and thrive in the damp English Weather.

Carniolan

These bees originally come from Middle Europe and are a popular choice among American beekeepers. they are known for increasing their numbers quickly and being extremely docile.

Caucasian

This type of honey bee is native to an area near the Caspian sea, in the foothill of the Ural Mountains. Not a very popular choice among beekeepers.

Russian

A fairly new breed of bee that is said to be resistant to mites and other health issues.

German

These were the first honey bees brought to the Americas. While there are many species of bees native to North America, there are no native honey bees. German bees were brought to the new world in the 17th century by explorers and settlers. These bees have several drawbacks to the backyard beekeeper and are not recommended.

What is the initial monetary investment involved?

The combined cost of bees, a hive and the necessary tools and protective gear should total between $500-600, as of this writing. You may be able to save some money by purchasing a starter kit or building your own hive. Using a top bar hive instead of a Langstroth Hive can save you a substantial sum of money.

Will I be stung?

Yes. That's is no way to avoid the occasional sting. This is why you don't want to keep bees if you are allergic to them. Being stung is nothing to worry about. To a person without bee allergies, a stung will cause little more than some minor swelling. The adverse reaction to stings tends to diminish the more a person is stung. Many veteran beekeepers feel almost nothing when stung. So yes, you will be stung and no, it's not that big of a deal.

How much honey can I expect to gather?

The amount of honey your bees will be able to produce is dependent on many factors and will vary somewhat from year to year. Things like weather, geographic location the amount of available food, the health of your colony all contribute to the amount of honey produced. It is safe to say, that if you have a healthy hive then you can expect more than enough honey for your needs every year. The average production for a single hive can be around 20-35 pounds.

Which type of Hive is best for the beginner?

The Langstroth Hive is recommended to those just starting out. It is the standard for beekeepers in most parts of the world and offers a simple, non-destructive way to harvest honey and maintain the hive.

The main disadvantages to the Langstroth hive are its price and size. While not overly large, a Langstroth type hive is considerably larger than a top bar type hive and requires a little more attention and maintenance. They are also more expensive.

A Top Bar Hive, while smaller, cheaper and simpler than the Langstroth produces less honey.

There is really no right or wrong hive, just one that is right for you and your situation. It is suggested that you read up on both types of hive and select one that fits into your space and budget. Chances are that you will eventually try both types of hive if you find yourself enjoying your bees.

Glossary

The following is a list of commonly used terms that you'll come across in you delve deeper into the world of beekeeping.

After Swarm - The first time a hive swarms in a year, it is called a primary swarm. If the hive swarms again, that swarm and any that come after it are called "After Swarms." The after swarm will contain a new virgin queen, in the primary swarm the mature queen leaves the hive.

Apiary - A group of hives in one area.

Apiculture - The study and practice of beekeeping.

Bee Bread - A mixture of nectar and pollen that is shaped into tiny balls and stored in the cells of a honeycomb. Bee bread is a source of food for the hive.

Brood Chamber - The section of the hive where the young bees are raised and allowed to mature.

Capping - A name given to the thin layer of bee's way that covers the cell in which it is stored.

Cell - a chamber in a honeycomb, it is hexagonal in shape and used to store honey, pollen or raise young in.

Cleansing Flight - The name given to what is essentially, the bees leaving the hive in a large group to use the bathroom.

Colony - The name given to a group of bees living in the same hive.

Comb - These are what the bees build inside the hive. The combs provide structural support to the hive and contain cells, which are used to store various things.

Fanning - The act of bees beating their wings together in order to lower the internal temperature of the hive.

Larva - The second stage of the bees life cycle

Package Bees - The standard way beekeepers get their bees. Package bees are a 2-5 pound screened box of bees that contains worker bees, drone bees, and an optional queen bee. They are traditionally shipped via the United States Postal Service.

Pheromones - A chemical with a distinctive odor which is emitted by bees and used for navigation and communication. It can best be pictured as a smell based telephone network.

Pupa - The third stage of a bee's life cycle

Propolis - A name given to tree and plant resins which are collected by worker bees and used in a similar fashion as glue. It is used to make minor repairs, seal splits and cracks - it is also known as bee glue.

Scout Bees - A type of worker bee that is responsible sources of food and a place for the colony to settle while swarming.

Smoker - A metal can in which a smoke producing fuel is burned. The beekeeper uses this smoke to confuse the bees and make them docile. This practice makes bee keeping safer and easier for both the keeper and the bees.

Super- A small box used to store excess honey produced by bees in a Langstroth hive.

Swarm- This is how bee colonies decide. Most of the worker bees and the queen leave the hive and seek to establish a new one in a different location. Swarming differs from Absconding, which is when the bees vacate the hive because of pets or other concerns.

Virgin Queen - A queen bee that has not mated.

Conclusion

Thank you again for reading this book!

I hope that this book was able to help you to gain a basic understanding of what is involved in raising your own bees.

The next step is to do some research regarding the legalities of keeping bees in your area and to gather your beekeeping supplies and prepare your property for your hive.

Finally, if you enjoyed this book, please take the time to share your thoughts and post a review on Amazon. It'd be greatly appreciated!

Thank you and good luck!

Chris

CHRISTOPHER SELBY

Copyright 2015

Copyright 2015 by Rach Helson LLC. All rights reserved.

Copyright 2015 By Nom De Plume

This document is geared towards providing exact and reliable information in regards to the topic and issue covered. The publication is sold with the idea that the publisher is not required to render accounting, officially permitted, or otherwise, qualified services. If advice is necessary, legal or professional, a practiced individual in the profession should be ordered.

From a Declaration of Principles which was accepted and approved equally by a Committee of the American Bar Association and a Committee of Publishers and Associations.

In no way is it legal to reproduce, duplicate, or transmit any part of this document ineither electronic means or in printed format. Recording of this publication is strictly prohibited and any storage of this document is not allowed unless with written permission from the publisher. All rights reserved.

The information provided herein is stated to be truthful and consistent, in that any liability, in terms of inattention or otherwise, by any usage or abuse of any policies, processes, or directions contained within is the solitary and utter responsibility of the recipient reader. Under no circumstances will any legal responsibility or blame be held against the publisher for any reparation, damages, or monetary loss due to the information herein, either directly or indirectly.

Respective authors own all copyrights not held by the publisher.

The information herein is offered for informational purposes solely, and is universal as so. The presentation of the information is without contract or any type of guarantee assurance.

The trademarks that are used are without any consent, and the publication of the trademark is without permission or backing by the trademark owner. All trademarks, photographs and brands within this book are for clarifying purposes only and are the owned by the owners themselves, not affiliated with this document.

About The Author

Christopher Selby lives in Colorado with his wife, Elizabeth, and their twin children, Jake, and Lily. In addition to raising and writing about bees, Christopher also enjoys making wine, gardening, and camping with his family. Like many authors, he is fond of cats.

Printed in Great Britain
by Amazon